"Smith's harrowing, tautly crafted long poem brings events of a century ago from shadow into light. To call this book 'unflinching' would be inaccurate, because it does flinch—as many readers need to and will flinch—at the stories it tells. Like few World War I poems since Wilfred Owen's, *Burden* asks that we face 'the old torment of the earth' and war's hasty disposal of those in its service. This is a book grounded in recovery, anger, and forgiveness." —BRIAN BARTLETT, author of *The Watchmaker's Table* and *Wanting the Day*

"The poetry of *Burden* exposes the brutality of a solider's OSI (operational stress injury) with dignity and poignancy." —LIEUTENANT-GENERAL (RET) THE HONOURABLE ROMÉO DALLAIRE

"Smith's spare poems expand beyond memory or memorial into the injustice at the core of all war." —BENJAMIN HERTWIG, author of *Slow War*

"*Burden* imprints our consciousness with the searing reality of a traumatized soldier executed for deserting the battlefield, and with the haunted yet epiphanic aftermath for a comrade assigned to the firing squad. Smith's service to those casualties of war and his dispatches to us, their inheritors, supplant dishonour with empathy, justice, and catharsis." —RICHARD LEMM, author of *Jeopardy* and *Shape of Things to Come*

ᎤᏂᏆ

OSKANA POETRY & POETICS

"A book grounded in recovery, anger, and forgiveness." —BRIAN BARTLETT

Burden

DOUGLAS BURNET SMITH

Douglas Burnet Smith

Burden

University of Regina Press

© 2020 Douglas Burnet Smith

All rights reserved. No part of this work covered by the copyrights hereon may be reproduced or used in any form or by any means—graphic, electronic, or mechanical—without the prior written permission of the publisher. Any request for photocopying, recording, taping or placement in information storage and retrieval systems of any sort shall be directed in writing to Access Copyright.

Printed and bound in Canada at Marquis. The text of this book is printed on 100% post-consumer recycled paper with earth-friendly vegetable-based inks.

Cover art: "Brodie Helmet" by cheapsoldier11shoes/Favpng.com

Cover and text design: Duncan Campbell, University of Regina Press

Editor: Jan Zwicky
Proofreader: Donna Grant

The text and titling faces are Arno, designed by Robert Slimbach.

Canada Council   Conseil des arts
for the Arts   du Canada

Canadä

creative
SASKATCHEWAN

Library and Archives Canada Cataloguing in Publication

Title: Burden / Douglas Burnet Smith.

Names: Smith, Douglas, 1949- author.

Identifiers: Canadiana (print) 20200272322 | Canadiana (ebook) 20200272918 | ISBN 9780889777729 (softcover) | ISBN 9780889777743 (PDF) | ISBN 9780889777767 (EPUB)

Subjects: LCSH: Burden, Herbert, 1898-1915—Poetry.

Classification: LCC PS8587.M526 B87 2020 | DDC C811/.54—dc23

10 9 8 7 6 5 4 3 2 1

UNIVERSITY OF REGINA PRESS
University of Regina
Regina, Saskatchewan
Canada S4S 0A2
TELEPHONE: (306) 585-4758
FAX: (306) 585-4699
WEB: www.uofrpress.ca
EMAIL: uofrpress@uregina.ca

We acknowledge the support of the Canada Council for the Arts for our publishing program. We acknowledge the financial support of the Government of Canada. / Nous reconnaissons l'appui financier du gouvernement du Canada. This publication was made possible with support from Creative Saskatchewan's Book Publishing Production Grant Program.

Nomanneslond
Middle English c. 1350

A piece of land outside the north wall of London, formerly used as a place of execution.

—*Oxford English Dictionary*

CONTENTS

1   **I**
Reg Smith
Pas-de-Calais, France
April 1915

11   **II**
Reg Smith
Shepreth Village Hospital
Cambridgeshire
May–June 1915

23   **III**
Reg Smith
Belgian Campaign
July 1915

33   **IV**
Reg Smith
Craiglockhart Hospital, Edinburgh
September–October 1915

57   **V**
Herbert Burden
Shot at Dawn Statue Unveiling
Alrewas, Staffordshire
August 2000

63   *Notes*
65   *Acknowledgements*

Some years ago I came into possession of a bundle of letters written by Lance Corporal Reginald Smith, a distant relative, letters that had been sent to his family in Canada from the front during World War I, the so-called Great War of 1914–18. Owing to standard military procedure, these letters were heavily redacted. It is thus hard to be certain, but it appears that Reginald Smith was ordered by his superiors to be part of the firing squad that executed Private Herbert Burden, a shell-shocked British soldier, for desertion. The letters also suggest that Smith was severely traumatized as a consequence.

Herbert Burden was seventeen at the time.

Over the course of the war, a total of 306 soldiers were shot by their own side for cowardice, desertion, or dereliction of duty. It took almost a century for the British government to recognize this practice as perfidious, and to pardon Burden and all the others executed for their so-called crimes. The pardon included the erection of a public memorial, a statue called *Shot at Dawn*, created by Andy DeComyn, and modeled on Herbert Burden.

Those who might have defied their superiors' orders to shoot a comrade risked execution themselves. Like Reginald Smith, they followed orders; and if they somehow managed to survive the war, they went on to live, as best they could, under the weight of their obedience.

The work of this book was not just to sift through mud-splattered letters and create a mimesis of terrible and terrifying events—and of one cruel and crucial event in particular—but to give voice and shape to the meditations of a ghost.

—DBS

I

REG SMITH

PAS-DE-CALAIS, FRANCE
APRIL 1915

Night-wiring. Dead silence,
    Support Trench.

A few yards away, spitting
    close, their trench.

And they knew: no ammunition.
    Showered in moonlight,

one of them climbed out, un-
    armed, yelled something

German at us, stile-stepped the bodies
    from his side, until he reached

ours. A death's-head skull
    glinted on his helmet, a clump

of mangled men away, not twenty paces.
    Through the periscope I could read

the motto on his belt-buckle: *Gott Mitt Uns.*
    He unbuttoned his trousers. He pissed

into an open mouth, a man I didn't want to know.
    No one spoke. No one breathed.

Whistling, he sauntered off. His comrades followed.
    Someone crawled up the duckboard,

removed the dead man's spectacles, shut
    the eyes and mouth, covered the face with dirt.

Moths, white moths, thousands
    flitting over the tortured field.

From behind their lines, mortars
    screamed in.

We ransacked the trench-store
    for gauze-pads and felt-bags.

Not enough, of course, to go around.
    The man who'd been feeding

the emptied Vickers fell,
    face-down in the mud.

Blown-out shoulder?
    I hoisted him up and saw:

a perfect hole in his forehead. Snaking
    over him, I couldn't angle myself

below the breastworks. Whatever hit
    threw me against the timbers,

and I felt disbelief flood my neck-veins.
    I was beginning to choke. To die

in a crump-hole.
    Beginning to know it.

❈

From above, and closing in, fast:
    daisy-cutter! Deafening

grunt of its plunge, hiss
    of the gas gong, and that high-pitched

compression: the dream
    you're floating in. Everything

flying, splintered loud and silent.
    You consist of pure

time-and-air, all things falling upside-
    down, toward the sky.

A French dawn
    the colour of trampled grapes.

❧

Coming to, grey light
 seeped into the muck

filling my eyes:
 pebbled dirt, grain-mealy.

Shell-bits
 barbed my mouth:

bubbled foam, blood-crust
 tickling each corner.

I *think* I remember
 the flash, and falling off the ridge

of limbs stiffened in the trench:
 a one-month veteran dragged

by his ankles through the mud. I heard
 the words *forgive me*, and I tried

to raise an arm—desperate to salute. Then
 an awful, buried belly-laugh.

My head surfaced beside a hand
 the laugh might have belonged to.

A hand glistening, wet from rain.
 The cleanest thing I'd ever seen.

Rats advanced,
    brown waves, like the trench-

water they skirred over. Slicked along
    the revetted boards,

slowing down for balance.
    You'd see them, individually,

tense and coil and make the leap
    from one board, one faceless man, to the next.

Gnawed sockets,
    gnawed bones. Sometimes

strings of hair smeared across raw scalp,
    or plain pulp, a half-eaten ear,

head half-visible above the mud.
    Asleep, we could hear

claw-scratch, teeth
    busy reducing

what was left of us,
    the Northumberland Fusiliers.

Up, and over. Each charge, one man implored
    God be with us, as if to say it just to be done

saying it. Every mad scramble I'd think—God's
    already here. He's been with us all along.

In the blood-sludge. In the guts worming out of that man
    cursing us from a stretcher,

rats surveilling him—the raw
    intelligence of their eyes.

God, the strains of a violin: sickeningly
    beautiful, from the enemy trench.

In the very word *enemy. Vimy. Arras. Pas-de-Calais.*
    God, the gun-bolt

shattering what was once a face.
    Two heads on monastery gate-posts

we marched past one evening.
    Pretending not to notice.

At the Dressing Station,
    I passed out

as they patched me up,
    triceps to wrist, horsehair

and parachute silk, gauze from a fresh corpse.
Left a good-sized drain-hole.

I do remember slow moaning,
    the man beside me in that rattle-

trap ambulance, and, sporadic, the chop
and spray back across the Channel.

Lorrie, gurney, echoing hallway. Lights
    dim, a rolling bed…

the mask descending toward my face.
    Counting backward. 100, 99, 98…

A distant voice whispering *Safe*.
Safe now, you're in Shepreth.

II

REG SMITH

SHEPRETH VILLAGE HOSPITAL
CAMBRIDGESHIRE
MAY–JUNE 1915

Things in that room discovered
    outlines in the dawn: daybed,

washbasin, pitcher. Crucifix
    in the mirror.

Window chair. Starched
    sheets and an arm

gift-wrapped in bandages, an offering
    to me, from the rest of me.

What *seemed* to be me.
    The day-nurse came in.

She put two fingers
    on my good wrist. Turned off

the night-light and daylight hurried
    across her lips as she smiled.

Careful, she folded my uniform.
    Silent, gentle, dutiful. Gone.

White ribbon
    pinned to the wall over my bed. *What?*

Through the window all morning, I watched a tree
 forming. Whoever I was, I was

weeping: I could still feel
 her fingers on my skin.

❅

Dream: Grace Street, cowering small
    in my father's arms. Veranda, thunderheads

rolling in off the prairie, lightning in threads, like
    hairs crackling on burnt skin:

the Manitoba sky. And when I woke again, still
    alone in that room, amplified over bird-calls

I heard a score of boots outside,
    crunching gravel. No unison march, but boot

grating on boot, an out-of-step crisscross
    of bumbling sincerity, trying not to fall, or

stumble into one another. Not even, God forbid,
    to *touch* one another. Like slow children

learning dance-steps.
    From the bed I could see heads

bobbing. "What's wrong with them?"
    The nurse said,

"There's nothing much wrong with that lot."
    And then, through her teeth, snapping

a bedsheet in the air, "Though certainly
    some are missing a spine." In time, I'd learn:

shell-shocked, they couldn't hold a thing
    in mind, not even cadence

from a snare-drum. On bright days
    they could manage a slow trudge.

❀

One man, a captain, had been an Oxford don, and crack shot. They called him, fondly, *Kraut*, or *Spy*.

"Full of useless information," he said, "but can't remember my own name," writing down, in a shaky hand, the meaning of my rank:

Lance Corporal—from *lancepesade*.
Old French through Old Italian,

lancia spezzata. "Supposedly, *superior soldier*. Literally," he said, "*shattered lance*."

❦

They came to take him back. The front: so
    depleted, any nerve-wracked scarecrow would do.

A Crossley arrived, and he climbed in under the dark tarp.
    He waved. The nurses waved. Jaunty

Union Jacks and flimsy applause. One nurse wept.
    The men left behind looked down at the gravel.

I sat in a chair in the sun. Rooftop doves gurgled.
    Spasmodic wings. The Crossley pulled away.

❊

Through the window, a boyish face
    from the crossing. Standing alone, arms

wrapped around himself, shivering as if the air were arctic.
    They'd been treating him with electric current—

phantom blindness—you could see red indentations
    on his temples. I sat across from him, once, at a table

in the improvised mess. He told me his name, staring
    at nothing about ten feet away. Burden.

He showed me the discharge report
    with his false age:

>   *Shepreth Village Hospital: June 8, 1915.*
>   *Burden, Herbert.*
>   *Age: 19.*
>   *Citizenship: British.*
>   *Private, Northumberland Fusiliers.*
>   *14th Service Battalion.*
>   *O-3832.*
>   *Cognitive Impairment: Partially Recovered*
>   *(Tremors, Occasional Stutter).*
>   *Recommendation: Ready to Resume All Duties (Monitored).*

He knocked over an empty glass,
dropped a plate, on purpose, I was sure.

The next week they sent him back.
A night wire-cutter.

❦

After all the men were gone, nurses gathered
    on lawns sloped to a stream—

audible, it seemed, only at dusk. Reclined
    on blankets, they smoked cigarettes, balancing

white shoes on their toes.
    Uncanny. Not a single shoe

fell from a single foot, no matter
    how I prayed for one to fall,

just to see a sliver of uninjured flesh.
    One night, a hand

slid along my back, and down. If I hadn't
    pushed my face into the bed

I might have felt
    the pulse of desire,

body lost in the dark. Darker
    than any room should be.

Did they mean anything? The roses
   on the night-table, the droplet

spider on a high-reaching petal? The flame
   of the candle? Luster

of web-lace in the corner candlelight
   cast there? Did the cross

above the bed signify anything
   more than the bed itself? Than the chair?

Than any common thing in that room?
   Did it mean something

when caissons rumbled past
   and the cross

wobbled? A loose nail
   holding it in place.

❋

And the white ribbon?—I asked,
    sure my obsequies had begun.

The nurse laughed. "*Milk cure, my dear.*"
    And handed me my release:

> *Shepreth Village Hospital: June 20, 1915.*
> *Smith, Reginald.*
> *Age: 21.*
> *Citizenship: Canadian.*
> *Lance Corporal, Northumberland Fusiliers.*
> *14th Service Battalion.*
> *O-3324.*
> *Cognitive Impairment: None.*
> *Right Arm Capacity: Whole & Useful.*
> *Recommendation: Ready to Resume All Duties*
>   *(Unmonitored).*

III

REG SMITH

BELGIAN CAMPAIGN
JULY 1915

Illegible signatures sent me back.
    Whole & Useful. And terrified.

Thirty-one days against a shattered wall, Hooge Sector:
    every face, even the youngest, shockingly

aged. Many more, gone—
    into the old torment of the earth.

❧

We came out of woods to a breathless
    town, Wieltje, cindered with men:

Dubliners, all of them, wiped out, chlorine smoke
    drifting homeless over smashed beams, roofs

crushed, piecemeal migrations thickening
    and thinning, and, breaking through, the sun

eyeing grotesque trophies:
    mouths open like bells, silence

leaking out. So that the dead were...
    The dead were nothing but the dead.

One step to the next, they'd collapsed—
    no more holding the world aloft. Yawning,

bored with it all. Or earnest, as though calling
    a child. And there *was* a child, farther on, beside

the waterless fountain. Pigeons made special use
    of the eyes. A little girl's eyes. (Skirt crumpled

above her legs, nothing there recognizable.)
    I sat against the fountain wall

facing the church and kicked at one of the birds.
    Its neck shone like spilled oil. I stared

 at what was left of the girl.
  The silence kept growing, and then

 the shriek of a gate, a young boy
  bolted out barefoot,

 waving arms and yelling, *Bosche! Bosche!*
  English! I yelled back.

He brushed past me, pointing
 up, sunlight glinting

on a helmet in the belfry.
 Someone aimed and fired.

The helmet fell hollow
 to the street. The boy disappeared

inside the church, re-appeared above
 some minutes later, heaved

the body of a Hun down to the cobbles.
 I walked over to inspect. On the man's

face—mild curiosity. A crow
 on the roof of the tower

peered down
 at the dead man, then

into the western sky, a dark pattern
    of others just like it approaching

like blind judgment. The boy walked out
    the church door, smirking, with the Hun's boots on.

❦

The C.O. wanted an aerial mast.
    He sent Burden to mount the cross

in what had been the nave. We watched
    his mud-caked boots dig into the elbows

of the outstretched arms of Christ.
    He was sweating big drops

onto the downcast face, bundled on his back
    the apparatus:

accumulators, dry cells, cord, coiled wires, earth mats.
    He reached up to tie the wires.

"Higher," the C.O. said. A friendly machine-gun burst
    from behind some rubble startled Burden. He

tumbled, splitting the side of his head open
    on the spike in our Lord's marble feet.

✠

Outside Wieltje we found the stream
    that had fed the mill near Shell Trap Farm.

With my hands I scooped water. I watched
    my face undulate, go still.

Burden used his helmet as a bowl. Poured
    cold water over his gashed head.

He turned into anonymous slivers. Water,
    courage, falling to the ground.

Slumped against headstones.
 A convoy edged by, and then—nothing at all. Hours

or days? We hadn't eaten in so long,
 had the L.C. made us count-off again

we'd have blown away over the fetid ground.
 Burden said he could see

a skull on every grave: his brief nightmare.
 Everything had become posthumous.

IV

REG SMITH

CRAIGLOCKHART HOSPITAL, EDINBURGH
SEPTEMBER–OCTOBER 1915

Others mocked his jitters. I'd talked Burden's wind-ups
    down for weeks. In lulls, I sketched placid scenes:

Canada, the vast plains, places he should know.
    But, as we fidgeted in the graveyard,

he just walked away. Burden. He stood, looked down
    at me, shook his head, and limped off

toward the trees. I thought: he's gone to relieve
    himself. Orders came to move out. Burden

didn't come back. I called after him, until
    the last uniform disappeared, then ran to catch up.

On the march from Bellewaarde Ridge, in the singing,
    Burden's voice was the absent soprano. Glimpsed

in a furrow, a terrified hare's eyes
    were Burden's. Two days gone,

I was accused of conniving.
    (I'd kept silent about his flight.)

I told them: he'll be back. Hadn't others
    done the same—scuttled off, hid

in some blasted farmhouse, thawing out
    their fear? Redcaps found him miles away,

spike-bozzled, shivering in his skivvies in a shepherd's
    hillside hut, surrounded by a family of cats.

Officers insisted: *He must be shot.*
    Stops others skiving. Turn your back,

You invite the fooking Kaiser
    straight into Buckingham Palace.

Bloody-well rapes his way there.
    No use arguing Burden ran off

to discover how empty he was,
    how empty we'd all become.

My letter of invitation: "Dear Lord Kitchener,
    your presence is requested in Poperinghe

(with stops at Ypres and Loos, long enough to count to 70,000)
    at the place of execution of Private Herbert Burden,

shot at dawn for desertion. Do come. See where excellent
    English bullets wedded him, confettied

him. Ravished him. Undid each brass button,
    ripped open the tunic, his chest

a torch lighting the lane
    to Coward's Heaven. Go on. Fondle

the post where a bugle sounded the hymn
    you hummed, signing the announcement to his mother."

✠

Some day I'll have to return. To that place.
    That place of—what, exactly? Undoing?

Here, I badger the talking cure
    across the page, scribbling a sad path back.

Pitiful row of knuckles on paper—hunched
    away from me, chagrinned, as if to say, *Not Guilty*—

we had our orders. The sound they make
    pushing the pen-nib is the sound

wind made in scant light, Burden's final hours:
    ten-minute trial, two-minute deliberation. Sentence.

Bath, shave, haircut. Clean uniform, hot meal.
    Bottle of rum. Morphine. Chaplain-and-Bible.

They led him out, drunk, stumbling,
    tied him to the post at the ankles, at the chest.

Where the L.C. pinned a piece of dirty
    muslin, the colour of a derelict beach. *Aim*

here! He poked Burden with his baton.
    As if we needed instruction. As if

our fingers didn't already know—stiff
    with the cold, the damp—

to squeeze slowly, between
       breaths, our parade of small mists.

Smoke from ten muzzles,
       cartridges spiraling out

toward that ragged blotch,
       3,000 feet per second.

I squeezed the trigger.
>   Birds panicked,

ten faces against the weak light.
>   The Sergeant's "insurance" Webley

against Burden's temple
>   flared.

❧

The birthmark on his throat, a bright purple
    medal. The obliteration of it.

(Someone aimed too high.) The pinched voice
    of Chaplain, the wind-bitten words:

The Lord… my Shepherd… I shall not…
    The jig Burden's feet danced

as the bullets hit, every one of us praying
    ours was the blank.

He saluted the firing line:
    muzzles and visible breath. Dead

cigarette stuck to lower lip, his head
    jerking up, and back, cigarette

falling. Emaciated village boys
    who'd been watching, waiting,

darted to his feet.
    Fighting for it.

What's left? Misery of repetition, trying to find
    truth in a story that's always changing, always

the same—like the moth compelled to return
    to this lamp, the archive of its brief

dumb life stored in every frayed scrape
    across the shade. Forever the same,

never the same. Each pass more
    frenetic. Faint detonations in its wings.

Chaplain offered the blindfold. Burden stared
    at the ten of us, in formation, waiting

for the order. He asked for a cigarette. The smoke
    made a patchy veil in front of his face.

The cigarette died, the smoke
    drifted off. He should have looked

hopeless, that desolate fuse
    stuck to his bottom lip.

But his face burned
    with providence, seeing beyond

orders, duty, trigger fingers, all the way
    to some moment years ahead:

one of us standing at a window,
    cup and saucer in hand, gazing

into the overcast, listening
    to the faint ticking of a clock

from a farther room, hearing
    the hour chime as we place the saucer

on the windowsill. Then,
    just as the shuddering

in the shoulders begins
    to travel down to the hands, and persists,

someone comes up behind us, reaches
    her arms around our chest and says, not

unkindly but firmly, "It's all right.
    That's it. Relax. It's over now. Finish your tea."

✤

We aimed our guns at him, this waif,
    a schoolboy who should have been

bored to death in some dismal classroom, squinting
    at crimped handwriting on a blackboard,

names from tedious years
    carved into the desks,

ink-smeared loops and grooves:
    Nigel, Stella, Austin. Herbert.

We pleaded, *Burden, take the blindfold.*
    He shook his head and uttered

no, the word
    piercing every conversation,

no matter what the subject,
    no matter where you are, or what you've become,

whatever life you've gone back to, if you've aimed
    a Ross MK II rifle at a schoolboy,

one of your eyes closed, the other
    honing in on the white patch

pinned over the valves of his seventeen-
    year-old heart. The truth is a sad cliché:

the rest of your days his whisper
    floats in everything—

traffic in the street, brakes
    of the morning bus,

doors of the evening bus.
    You mount the stairs,

sit, and squinch at newsprint
    in dim light. And when you think

you've escaped, downing another pint
    in the pub, suddenly

it's there: released lever, spigot hiss—
    you're sure the ale has shattered the glass,

you're sure everyone can hear
    his whisper. It ricochets

off that long, wavy mirror
    behind the bar, the mirror

in which you observe
    your bewildered face,

crowded in among the others,
    billowing into the face

of someone else, someone who,
   because this is a cliché, is at once you

and not you, "strangely familiar." You can feel
   the trigger against your finger. You hold

your breath. You take aim at the mirror.
   You close one eye and squeeze.

❀

After they'd folded him
    into a grave dug too quickly,

a grave too small, even for Burden,
    and covered him over too quickly, because

it was sleeting, and the men digging
    did not want to get any wetter,

I was ordered, along with two others,
    to round up the goats that had appeared

at mess tents scrounging for food. Rations had run low.
    (Supply lines? Choked off.) We followed pebble

scat under stunted trees, scrambled over
    a hill and found ourselves at Shell Trap Farm

(which they now made us call Mouse Trap Farm
    for morale's sake, after the Dubliners cock-up).

A lone crow clawed and tugged
    at something in ankle-deep muck.

Then, soaked meadow-
    grass and matted leaves, until

the gravel of a farmyard and deep
    weather-beaten troughs, half-

empty, whose brackish water three goats,
    staring at us as we approached,

could no longer reach just by leaning over.
   They had to leap and balance spindly

dung-stained legs on the edges
   of the troughs, and drink, almost

tipping, then jump down
   backward, as if completing

a circus trick. It was easy. One bullet each.
   We tied hooves

to a long branch and shouldered them.
   A wind came up and slapped leaves

on our faces. Returning—terrible rain, wind-
   driven slant. We were drenched, almost

crippled when we reached the sprawl of camp.
   Skinned and gutted, the goats roasted

over a meagre fire. Not much flesh
   on the bones. Dry and tough.

I could see Burden's muddy grave
   disintegrating in the rain.

I ate.
   No taste at all.

I wake up, wicker chair under the trees.
    A window in nurses' quarters bright.

Perhaps it's late. Perhaps early,
    I can no longer tell. But someone,

someone's there, and the pale Scottish autumn
    sky is sublime. In the distance

a man pedals over the long hill,
    leans over the bars, pushing hard

to make it, weaving in and out
    of twilight.

And there, in the ocean's half-light,
    I see myself again, landing

at Cherbourg, dressed,
    you might say, to kill: khaki tunic,

pay-book breast pocket, rifle patches
    sewn in (no chafing from bandolier).

Peaked cap, tight
    leather-strapped chin,

brass fittings each side, two fussy
    gold buttons securing them. Puttees

at the ankles, puttees around the calves.
    Ammunition boots: hobnail

soles, brown (enlisted men, black), steel-plated
    heel. Left and right ammunition pouches,

75 rounds each, left and right braces,
    my bayonet frog,

my entrenching pick handle, its head
    safe in the web cover; water-bottle, haversack,

large pack, great coat folded inside.
    Rank—right upper sleeve,

Good Conduct stripes below. Stitched
    under left flap of lower tunic,

the First Field Dressing shields
    the small photo signed *Love, L_____*.

Squatting near me in a corner of the craft,
    a very young man, a boy really, throwing up.

❧

Dear Mater & Pater,
   Please do not worry about me.

The discharge from my ears has stopped,
   and though the ringing in the right ear

is still there, it is decidedly less bothersome
   than before. I do not know when Dr. Rivers

will decide that I am fit enough to return
   to the front, but I am keen to be

alongside the boys again. Winter is nearly upon us,
   and I pray it will be all over soon.

Your loving son,
   Reg

At the desk, writing home—
    and in he comes, shuffling across the room

like some clueless thief, stooping by the lamp,
    drooping to the bed. The weight

in his face. I say it. I say
    his name.

Because he asks me to.
    He lies down, closes his eyes, and listens.

The room fills with his name,
    his wound, simple breathing.

Suddenly there, then
    suddenly not. I go on surveying the sky,

one untroubled thing worth looking at
    in this long, short life. I've noticed

how a single cloud
    will desert the others, and float off.

How the other clouds
    don't seem to care.

V

HERBERT BURDEN

SHOT AT DAWN STATUE UNVEILING
ALREWAS, STAFFORDSHIRE
AUGUST 2000

Almost a hundred years it took for this? How caring. How... kind.
I'm quite tired. *Pardon me.*
It's wrong, the statue, really.
First, it's missing the fag in my mouth. That's essential.
Second, I *watched* them do it. I *refused* the blindfold.
I can remember how strangely slow that little spool of time-running-out unwound.
Far off, behind the line of men. Purple spreading into darkness.
A gull flew over, a blot of gauze and ash.
A rumble answered rumbling, somewhere in the distance.
Reg Smith looked down at the ground. Then raised his rifle, aiming.
One last thing. For the record:
I stood there, tied to the post. Just before they fired, and the fag fell at my feet, Chaplain whispered in my ear.
Have no fear. The world is always ending.
As if I should care. About the stupid world.
I saluted. I pissed myself.
Again, he whispered.
Something else I couldn't understand.

NOTES

Page 7
Northumberland Fusiliers. The second-largest infantry battalion of World War I, also known as *The Pioneers*. This regiment took part in almost every major battle on the Western Front from 1915 to 1918.

Page 30
Shell Trap Farm. On May 24, 1915, the German army launched an attack near this farm on Allied lines, using the largest amount of chlorine gas to date. All 666 men in the Second Battalion of the Royal Dublin Fusiliers died. It was renamed Mouse Trap Farm by the Allies in an attempt to erase the memory of the massacre and to boost morale.

Page 31
L.C. A casual abbreviation for "Lieutenant Colonel." It is used in this sense also on page 39.

Page 33
Craiglockhart Hospital. A famous "shell-shock" facility near Edinburgh, which treated psychiatric casualties as well as those who had been physically maimed. Patients included Wilfred Owen and Siegfried Sassoon.

Page 38
Lord Kitchener. British Secretary of State for War, 1914–1916.
Poperinghe. A town in Belgium, the gateway to the battlefields of Ypres and Loos. It was alternately occupied by Allies and Germans several times throughout the war.
Coward's Heaven. See Revelation 21:8.

Page 55
Dr. Rivers. William Halse Rivers, who developed the "talking cure" for shell-shock patients at Craiglockhart Hospital.

ACKNOWLEDGEMENTS

Thank you to Irene Rowlin, for the letters of Reg Smith, RIP to you both; to K.B., for the musical wit and sincerity; to Jan Zwicky, for such a deep commitment to this book, which ventured beyond bestowing upon it incomparable editorial acumen, toward a faith in the idea of continuing reparations for those who have been crushed by war and unjustly judged by history. Huge thanks to the Oskana board, for meticulous stewardship, and to the entire team at U of R Press. And to Sole, Gala, and Juana, immeasurable gratitude for being my power supply.

Douglas Burnet Smith is the GG Award–nominated author of *Voices from a Farther Room* and, most recently, *White Corvettes*. *Burden* is his seventeenth book of poetry. He divides his time between Athens, Greece, and Atlantic Canada, where he teaches in the English Department at St. Francis Xavier University in Antigonish, Nova Scotia. For a complete list of his works, visit douglasburnetsmith.com.

ᐅᓄᏃᇋ

OSKANA POETRY & POETICS
BOOK SERIES

Publishing new and established authors, Oskana Poetry & Poetics offers both contemporary poetry at its best and probing discussions of poetry's cultural role.

Jan Zwicky—*Series Editor*
Randy Lundy—*Acquisitions Editor*

Advisory Board

Roo Borson
Robert Bringhurst
Laurie D. Graham
Louise Bernice Halfe

Tim Lilburn
Daniel David Moses
Duane Niatum
Gary Snyder

For more information about publishing in the series, please see:
www.uofrpress.ca/poetry

PREVIOUS BOOKS IN THE SERIES:

Measures of Astonishment: Poets on Poetry,
presented by the League of Canadian Poets (2016)

The Long Walk, by Jan Zwicky (2016)

Cloud Physics, by Karen Enns (2017)

The House of Charlemagne, by Tim Lilburn (2018)

Blackbird Song, by Randy Lundy (2018)

Forty-One Pages: On Poetry, Language and Wilderness,
by John Steffler (2019)

Live Ones, by Sadie McCarney (2019)

Field Notes for the Self, by Randy Lundy (2020)

CANADIAN LITERATURE / POETRY / WWI

$4.99

"The poetry of *Burden* exposes t[...]
of a soldier's OSI (operational st[...]
with dignity and poignancy."
— GENERAL ROMÉO DALLAIRE

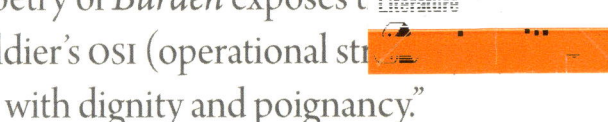

Burden is a book-length sequence of poems that swirls around the brutal death of Private Herbert Burden, who was shot for desertion during World War I. He was one of hundreds so executed. It is now understood that many of these men committed no crime, but were suffering from PTSD. Burden's story is told in the voice of Lance Corporal Reginald Smith, a distant relative of the author. Corporal Smith's fate becomes entwined with Burden's: having befriended Burden, Smith is ultimately ordered to be a member of the firing squad.

Douglas Burnett Smith's account is an object lesson in why poetry matters. It takes us to places even the best journalism cannot reach.

"*Burden* imprints our consciousness with the searing reality of a traumatized soldier executed for deserting the battlefield, and with the haunted yet epiphanic aftermath for a comrade assigned to the firing squad. Smith's service to those casualties of war and his dispatches to us, their inheritors, supplant dishonour with empathy, justice, and catharsis." —RICHARD LEMM, author of *Jeopardy*

"Smith's spare poems expand beyond memory or memorial into the injustice at the core of all war." —BENJAMIN HERTWIG, author of *Slow War*

DOUGLAS BURNET SMITH is the author of sixteen books of poetry. He teaches in the English Department at St. Francis Xavier University in Antigonish, Nova Scotia.

ᐅᓄᐸ
OSKANA POETRY & POETICS

University of Regina Press